STARS

By S.L. Hamilton

VISIT US AT
WWW.ABDOPUBLISHING.COM

Published by ABDO Publishing Company, 8000 West 78th Street, Suite 310,
Edina, MN 55439. Copyright ©2011 by Abdo Consulting Group, Inc. International
copyrights reserved in all countries. No part of this book may be reproduced
in any form without written permission from the publisher. A&D Xtreme™ is a
trademark and logo of ABDO Publishing Company.

Printed in the United States of America, North Mankato, Minnesota.
112010
012011

 PRINTED ON RECYCLED PAPER

Editor: John Hamilton
Graphic Design: Sue Hamilton
Cover Design: John Hamilton
Cover Photo: European Southern Observatory
Interior Photos: A. Fujii (ESO)-pgs 10 & 11; ESO-pg 1; ESO/S. Brunier-pgs 2 & 3;
NASA-pgs 4, 5, 6, 7, 8, 11, 12, 13, 16, 17, 18, 19, 20, 21, 22, 23, 24, 25, 26, 27, 28, 29,
30, 31, 32; NOAO/AURA/NSF-pgs 8, 9; Photo Researchers-pgs 14 & 15

Library of Congress Cataloging-in-Publication Data

Hamilton, Sue L., 1959-
  Stars / S.L. Hamilton.
    p. cm. -- (Xtreme space)
  ISBN 978-1-61714-741-8
  1. Stars--Juvenile literature. I. Title.
  QB801.7.H36 2011
  523.8--dc22
                              2010041218

CONTENTS

XTREME

Stars, like our Sun, have lives. They are born, go through several phases, and then die. This takes billions of years. Some stars are 1,000 times smaller than our Sun. These are dwarf stars. Others are supergiants, 100 to 1,000 times bigger than our Sun.

STARS

"When you look at the stars and the galaxy, you feel you are not just from any particular piece of land, but from the solar system." ~Laurel Clark

STARS

A star begins as a cloud of gas and dust called a nebula. Over millions of years, gravity and other forces cause the gas and dust to compress. The matter is packed so tightly that nuclear fusion begins, causing heat and light.

ARE BORN

The Carina Nebula is a pillar of dust and gas. It is an area filled with new star formations.

Types of Nebulas

Nebulas are immense collections of gas and dust. If a nebula shines because of light from nearby stars, it is called a reflection nebula. An emission nebula glows because its gas is energized by stars within it. A dark nebula is a dust cloud so tightly packed that it blocks visible light, and appears to be a dark blob in space.

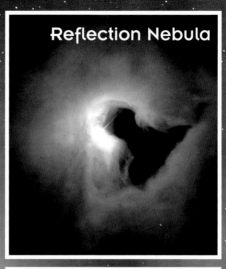

Reflection Nebula

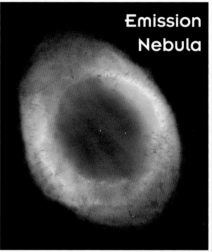

Emission Nebula

The Horsehead Nebula is
a well-known dark nebula.

MAIN SEQUENCE

A main sequence star is a young-to-middle-aged star. It is at a point in its life where it converts hydrogen into helium through nuclear fusion. Most stars, including the Sun and nearby Alpha Centauri, are main sequence stars.

Alpha Centauri

STARS

Most main sequence stars glow yellow. They are known as yellow dwarf stars. But the hotter they are, the brighter they appear. The star Sirius glows about 70 times brighter than the Sun. It is a white dwarf star.

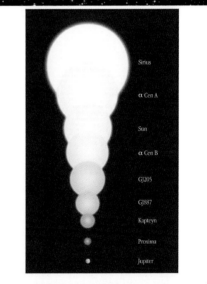

Sirius

α Cen A

Sun

α Cen B

GJ205

GJ887

Kapteyn

Proxima

Jupiter

Relative Sizes of the Alpha Centauri Components and Other Objects

Xtreme Fact

Sirius is a star in the constellation Canis Major (the Great Dog). It is the brightest star in our night sky.

Red Dwarf Stars

Red dwarf stars are also a type of main sequence star. They are the most common type of star in the galaxy. A red dwarf is smaller, cooler, and dimmer than a yellow or white dwarf star.

A gas giant planet orbiting a red dwarf star.

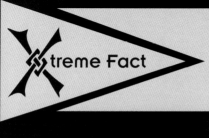

Xtreme Fact

Proxima Centauri is the nearest star to the Sun. It is a red dwarf. Its surface temperature is less than half that of the Sun.

Subgiant Stars

A subgiant star is a main sequence star that is running out of hydrogen at its core. It is nearing the end of its life cycle. Hydrogen fusion moves from its center to the shell surrounding its core. This makes the shell increase in size. The star also becomes somewhat brighter.

The star 79 Ceti is a yellow subgiant star. The planet 79 Ceti b orbits the star about once every 76 Earth days.

Red Giants and Supergiants

Betelgeuse

ORION

When an older star's hydrogen fuel is nearly used up, its core contracts. Its outer shell greatly expands, growing 10 to 100 times bigger than the Sun. Red giants are big and bright. They have a cooler surface temperature, which produces their red color. Supergiants are even larger stars. They can be up to 1,000 times bigger than the Sun.

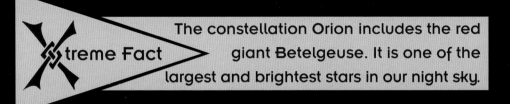

The constellation Orion includes the red giant Betelgeuse. It is one of the largest and brightest stars in our night sky.

Hypergiant Stars

Hypergiants are the biggest stars. One of these stars may be bigger than our solar system. The largest known star is a hypergiant named VY Canis Majoris. It is about 1,500 times bigger than the Sun and releases about 4 million times as much energy. Hypergiants are rare. At the end of their lives, they usually collapse and explode in a supernova.

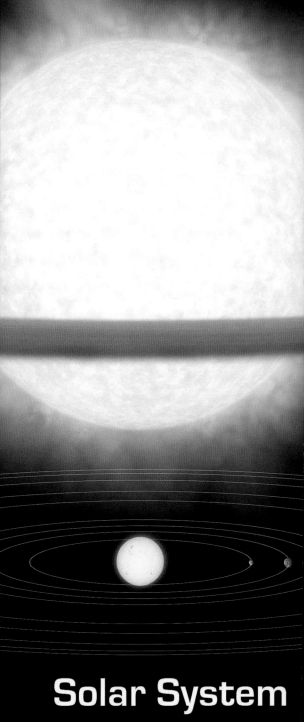

Solar System

Sun and planet sizes not to scale

Dust Ring around Hypergiant Star

Massive Star VY Canis Majoris

Xtreme Fact

VY Canis Majoris, a red hypergiant, is the biggest star known.

DYING

A star's life span depends on its size. Bigger, more massive, stars burn their fuel faster. Common main sequence stars, like the Sun, will live about 10 billion years. The Sun is now about halfway through its life span. It is about 4.5 billion years old.

Xtreme Definition

Planetary Nebula—When a star like the Sun uses up its fuel, a shell of gas is ejected, leaving behind a white dwarf. Early astronomers thought the gas looked like planets.

STARS

The Helix Nebula is a planetary nebula.

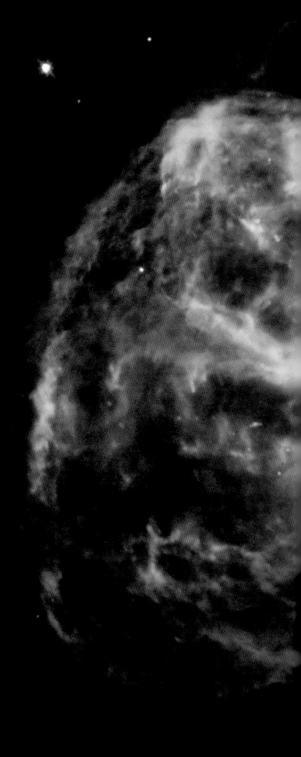

White and Black Dwarfs

When a main sequence star like the Sun runs out of nuclear fuel, it blows away its outer layers and collapses to a small, dense core called a white dwarf. Eventually, white dwarfs lose all their energy and cool down into black dwarfs.

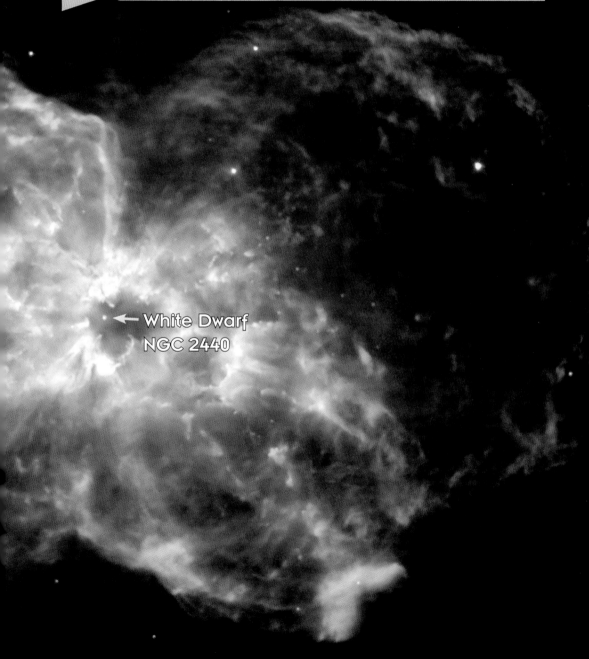

"The star (NGC 2440) is ending its life by casting off its outer layers of gas, which formed a cocoon around the star's remaining core." ~NASA.

Xtreme Quote

← White Dwarf
NGC 2440

GOING

When a massive star dies, it results in a supernova explosion. Immense gravitational forces give the explosion its energy. For a short time, supernovas can be as bright as 100 million Suns, brighter than an entire galaxy. Supernovas are rare. They happen about once every century in galaxies like ours, the Milky Way.

SUPERNOVA

Kepler's Supernova was first
seen in 1604. It is the last
supernova to have been
observed in our galaxy.

NEUTRON STARS

A neutron star is a small, intensely dense core of material left behind after a supernova. A teaspoon full of a neutron star might weigh as much as all the people on Earth!

AND PULSARS

If a neutron star rapidly rotates and emits pulses of energy that can be detected from Earth, it is called a pulsar.

A rapidly
rotating pulsar
in the Crab Nebula.

BLACK

After a supernova, sometimes a star's remaining core is so dense that gravity causes it to collapse further. It forms a black hole. It is a point in space with such intense gravity that even light cannot escape. Scientists study these invisible objects by observing how light and other space objects behave around suspected black holes.

HOLES

"The black hole teaches us that space can be crumpled like a piece of paper into an infinitesimal dot..." ~John Wheeler, Physicist

Xtreme Quote

THE

Galaxy
Stars, gas, and dust held together by gravity. Our solar system is part of the Milky Way Galaxy.

Gas Giant
A huge planet made mostly of gases. There are four gas giants in our solar system: Jupiter, Saturn, Uranus, and Neptune. Many other gas giants have been found circling other stars.

Hydrogen
The lightest and most plentiful gas in the universe. Stars are mostly made of hydrogen. The Sun is about 75 percent hydrogen.

Infinitesimal
A very tiny size. An amount approaching zero.

National Aeronautics and Space Administration (NASA)
A U.S. government agency started in 1958. NASA's goals include space exploration, as well as increasing

GLOSSARY

people's understanding of Earth, our solar system, and the universe.

Neutrons
A part of an atom that has a neutral (neither positive nor negative) electrical charge. A neutron star is one that has collapsed onto itself and is made only of neutrons.

Nuclear Fusion
A reaction that takes place when two lighter atoms combine to form a heavier atom. For example, in a star, two hydrogen atoms combine to form helium, a heavier atom. This process results in huge amounts of energy being released.

Solar System
A star and all the planets and other objects in space that orbit it. Our solar system includes the Sun, eight planets, dwarf planets, asteroids, and other space objects.

INDEX